ELISABETH MURAWSKI

Voyage to the End

SurVision Books

First published in 2026 by
SurVision Books
Dublin, Ireland
Reggio di Calabria, Italy
www.survisionmagazine.com

Cover image: *The Landing* by Leigh Dyer
Seafront near Denmark Place, Hastings, East Sussex

ISBN: 978-1-912963-64-5

Acknowledgments

Grateful acknowledgment is made to the editors of the following, in which some of these poems, or versions of them, originally appeared:

Apalachee Review: "A Musical Offering"
City Celebration 1976 (District of Columbia Bicentennial Commission, 1977): "Self-Portrait"
Crazyhorse: "It Has to Be Three Oranges"
Elixir: "Voyage to the End"
Folio: "Midsummer Mountain" and "Sorrow's End"
Higginsville Reader: "Karma Accelerating"
Illuminations: "On a Line from D. H. Lawrence"
The Journal of Religious Concern: "Breaking the First Commandment"
Laurel Review: "Greek Urn that I Am"
Literary Review: "Painting Found in the Lap of a Poem" and "Nerves"
Madison Review: "Obsessions"
North American Review: "Ode to Blanche DuBois"
Poet and Critic: "To a Mad Woman Poet"
The Poet Upstairs (ed. by Judith Ortiz Cofer, Pinata Books, 2012): *"Deed"*
Poetry Project Journal (Tupelo Press): "The One with Violets in Her Lap"
Potomac Review: "In All Things Love"
Shades of Grey: "A Place to Be Taken To"
Shenandoah: "Night Thoughts"
South Carolina Review: "Desolate"
South Dakota Review: "Wishless"
Verse Daily: "Voyage to the End"
Washington Review: "Rue" and "Magellan, Intensely"
Whose Woods These Are (ed. by Karren L. Alenier; The Word Works, 1983): "Sappho Rap"
Wordwrights: "Anniversary Poem" and "Mood"

For Jeanne Sorrentino

CONTENTS

Ode to Blanche DuBois

Me and Blanche
slink center stage
through a curtain of beads.

We hike up our gowns and shine
like tinsel from tossed out
Christmas trees.

In rooms smudged with pink
neon light
we lose our zero selves

in artful beaux.
Each morning, we tiptoe home
from the cold.

We sing in the tub.
We slip into silk kimonos
and smoke. Stars

we didn't have to make up
string us along.
We hold on tight to the string.

To a Mad Woman Poet

Who stole your rabbit's foot,
pushed you under virgin ladders,
dried your skin of flowers under lamps?

Who sewed your stuffed host on plush,
then made you genuflect
before the unidentified lump in your breast?

In your verses you pay back the sports.

You remember the doctors' small heads
nosegayed over your bed,
their glances trapped.

You are certain they made you dance
on a lightning table.

When you splashed to the floor, hot fish,
you heard cook warn the rubber children
to stay away from your bones.

You never did love cats.

Now your soul lies honed
on a frayed bed of lettuce.

Your eyes are strapped in newsprint
with your spine.

Quite close
you hear a young rabbit halt.

In your leafy keep you tremble...
for luck!

Breaking the First Commandment

What do my hands create?
A monarchy in long thrones,
a court of ants on cards,
a granite beard, hawthorn
after rain, and two fires.

Space is the Capitol,
the black marketplace where
beggars in a hurry to die
shoot the scales like stars.

And there on the corner,
slouching on the lamppost,
my brain of angels
notches wood,
looking up
a spiral of smoke,
cars fled, bars
of morning
on the awning,
my head an apple
for the arrow.

Look down:
the street is covered
with curls of wood,
rococo at his feet,
the gilt watch drawn,

the appointment book
neat crows.

Wind pokes holes
in the curtains
twelve o'clock high.

The bow spreads,
flies me to my
graven image.

On a Line from D. H. Lawrence

One glance, and I was Frieda
on the train, my gold cross

useless. The room fell away,
lanterns in our hands. Bison

and aurochs shimmered
on the walls of a cave,

beauty in motion.
Everything starts from us.

A twinge, yes, a flutter.
Lilacs in winter.

My eyes glittered
like the scales of a fish

attracting the albatross
that glides

down a current of air,
wings locked like a switchblade.

Magellan, Intensely

Crossing time with light
to demonstrate
an advent in the street

hungry to learn the difference
each world makes
to chase the mountain's wave

read what I say
in your breath shaping
a night of new wind

still sails lapping
in the backs of our eyes
both sides of the equator.

Anniversary Poem

I spread a white sheet
over straw where the moonlight
can see it

and then another sheet,
folded back.

Undressing, I hear
Beethoven's Seventh in my head,
I keep rehearsing

what to say to you,
awkward
as any moonwalker.

I take your hand and press it
to my heart.

We sit and look,
the silence

catching in our throats.
The straw roars
and whispers.

Crows

They cruise the newly planted seed
hawking their need
with the urgency of chainsaws.

I stuff straw
into a pair of trousers and a coat
but they do not scare.

Their mincing delegation
struts as if at court.
Their velvet contract

does not run out. They sit
as if at prayer,
bleak obituaries

from the jet plane
of Eurydice, flashing bitter
diamonds from the blacktop.

Painting Found in the Lap of a Poem

What I mean to say
is that the sweat
on a bottle of beer
the first drag on a cigarette
after we are quiet

is lighted sky
following a storm

is nakedness

is
this peach-tinged room

Billie Holiday
died in

is the tree I'd like to buy
outside your window

and what I'd do with it.

Night Thoughts

We have drifted too far south
from the equator.
I can feel the ice form
through the middle of the night.

We must be near an island
with its normal hazards
of isolated life.

A bird repeats its maddening note,
locked in this frieze.

I say to myself
certainly I hadn't expected
the blow struck in anger.
These things happen.
Shocking experiences can be accepted.

Then what does this do to my reason?
And why am I taking off my clothes?

Sappho Rap

You! Shakespeare!
Yes, you!
Funky swain of West End,
Blue Boy!
Come see Sappho dance!

O.K. call me gold-digger.
I'm a real soul-miner,
with the sun in my forehead
and nuggets fooling my hands.

But shame! Dirty pool!
All that's left of me?
Fragments!
And look at you—
Kismet—
captured alive!

I tell you Mister S.,
my little pieces
incomplete,
are my pure jazz!

What's left to dream
when it's hooked and eyed,
zipped or tied,
plain on paper?

I am elusive,
black negligee,
firefly.

Meaning filters through,
teasing in those bits of skin.

My gold is yours—
chased from the same vein,
the same divine.

So don't stumble on your nose.

Hustle up some soft shoes
and come see Sappho dance!

I'll hold you close, Willy boy—
I'll tap the gaps!

Self-Portrait

The bride is upside
down, her dream
lost.

A window frames
a cow
in a field.

A hand unfolds
her head, the yards
of skin.

The nude
is red, the farm
is mad

for eggs, fresh
meat, a golden
pram.

Day and night
the manger
fills with cream.

Day and night
the miser winds
more string.

Till cubic sweat
descends
the threshing floor.

And tallith-laid,
she bites
to the legal skeleton.

In the middle of straw
sizzles a howl
round as a mother.

Down wind
the cow begins
a deep lowing.

Wisconsin Death Trip

I want to swear a warrant
for your hands.
Hipstroker,

I want you broken,
gladiator parts of you
scattered on the sand.

Better exiled to a sky-lab
polishing chrome,
whittling slabs of soap—

your own private Stonehenge.
I want you anywhere
but here:

wearing black as an afterthought,
leaving prints
on my glass-bottomed boat.

Greek Urn That I Am

I have met you before
in the taste of whiskey

on the precipice
where the wind goes
for a smoke.

There are trees
I never looked for
looking from your face.

I move to my toes
speaking to the dark
as if it were my sister

addressing vacancy
as if it were my house

and I am lying low
because I know I must tell you

where I keep my knives.

Deed

Where does it hurt
Judith asks with her eyes
Holofernes

ignoring
the warmth on her hands
the May of life
the ooze

on the sword’s blade

staggering
through layers of gauze
into the night’s chill

swaying
as she looks ahead
to the horizon’s light
hanging on
to the slip of morning

not asking for reasons
not running away
merely kneeling at the stream
and watching the water
run clear

It Has to Be Three Oranges

When I first saw the children
spaced out on the tube
what it looks like to be brain-dead
it was as if they had been born
genetically unsound
I saw myself alone in the house
watching sit-coms
legs wrapped in an afghan
I saw myself wiping sweat
from the back of my neck
as the ovaries shut down
and I ate the last of the three oranges
and no one had come to my
grandmother or grandfather
for help or wisdom or kindness
they had left no such legacy
in the cities of Europe or America
and I wondered why they called it
Agent Orange when oranges feed me
sweet distractions and give me courage
to climb into a bed half-taken
and to close my eyes in the dark.

Midsummer Mountain

It was a day we should never have climbed.
The air gave out. Our clothes
stuck to our skins, and we envied the swimmers
pressing on to the pool. Even the insects
were wise, lay low. But we persisted,
you out of commitment, I following,
unwilling to be left behind
dreaming at the foot of the mountain.

Winded but stubborn, we moved more slowly
to the crest, breath more precious
with altitude. At the summit
we lost the view. Through haze
I clung to the memory of that earlier
morning when, waking from soundest sleep,
at the same instant we flung our arms
about each other without
hesitation or plan, abandoned
as the first crush of blossoms
torn from spring, then placed
in a simple vase the color of jasper.

Rue

The detour I fear
leans in the door.
I undo a shirt.

The pirate's scar
shines
incredibly softly.

That slowly lovely
animal
bends my will.

High above the sea
I hear her singing.
The ghost of a romantic girl.

Mood

First touch was sweet
because there was distance,
impossibility.

I can still hate for it,
black and silver threads
giving way

to a place
above the water.

It was raining of course.
The plums all
ravaged to the south.

Nerves

In my own way
I kill a spider.
Now its legs curl
rapidly

to attention,
the body blacker
against
a spray of mimosa.

There is a drawing
inward
to the heart.

The One with Violets in Her Lap

She thinks
she's the cat's miaow,
my fair lady. Forget

about the bridge
falling down. That part's
old hat. She's the sort

who steals for sport
the plums I want.
I cannot forgive her

the flute player, hot
and available.
No summer's day, she.

More a red-tailed hawk
with beady little eyes
the color of silt.

I'd put her on a ship
leaving Crete
in stormy weather!

Desolate

Bleak evenings eat into the chairs.
Into the mattress, the floors,
where we twist our bodies home.

In your house of yellow walls,
love must be given reasons.
I have no words that will work. You

select your truth with fingers crossed
and many times burned. Here is the kiss
I might give to you dying. The ignorant

do what they do, cannot see the mystery
in the fire of opals, the broken
life of the sun. I tear

the patches from your uniform, entrust you
to enemy crossfire, pray for snow
to make everything white again.

Karma Accelerating

Only children know
what they are looking for.
—St. Exupery, *The Little Prince*

Our last night in the garden
the moon
steps down from a cloud
like a movie star
on a gangplank. Pure
theatre.

You will send me
playbills from West End,
a copy
of your passport photo
in a Beatles haircut.

I don dark glasses.
Rearrange the furniture
to soften
the denouement.

From the chaos of airports
you call
to gloss the truth.

I polish the silverware.
Play the Black Mass
of Scriabin. All this

to forget how I knelt
on the chilly walk, undid
your belt.

Starlings flapped
from the eaves,
gossiping.

Obsessions

While I've been reading "Threnody"
and crying for little Waldo
and then for my father
and then for Jack Kennedy
(it's that kind of poem)
you've been at the kitchen counter
chopping walnuts
dicing cherries and pineapple,
so intent on the genesis of fruitcakes
you seldom stop to talk
but do ask how old little Waldo was
when he died. I say "Four or five"
and then I sit in silence, thinking
the baking pans look like tiny coffins.

While you are spooning batter in,
to counteract the dirge, I
lean over and whisper to your shoulder:
"Wanna be seduced?"
                                    As if you hadn't
heard right, you say "Pardon?"
and I blush. The room
seems darker, smaller, colder.

When the sweet cakes are done,
you'll drench them in bourbon,
seal them, as if they were tombs,
for the Advent season. I stare
at your kitchen calendar

with its white New England barn
stark as a church. I think
of how you like to sleep on your back
with your heart unprotected.

A Musical Offering

Those sorrows clasped to your breast
stood between us like a rock
struck and struck against,

the spring I hoped for
never surfacing. I began to read
your silences like entrails.

It was time, yet I held back,
fledgling, the secret of flight
still a secret. I clung

to what I knew, promised
I would always remember,
a vow come back to pulse

like an unforgiving ghost
in the black wrist of space
without you.

Sorrow's End

Please forgive the lies
of admiration,
the passion to create
in you
an indebtedness.

Paddles lifting
in unison, the canal
gilded with pollen,
didn't we move
the canoe
swiftly as sign language?

I choose
to remember your stubby
fingers, good
with wood. Awkward
with hooks and eyes.

Mood, with Star

I wash in a cold shower,
in a lust for love
scraping my soul,

afterwards combing
and careful. I have been
tricked before—

after all, the lilies
of the field were really
wildflowers. Still,

I startle a bluejay
when I tell him
this is not God's place,

this scene of a choice
to be conceived
by death

and its partner. I am
pierced by no angel.
The abyss is my egg,

my embryo, my dear
sweet nothing
on the needle's edge.

Beating on its shell
to come through, shaping
the bones of a smile.

In All Things Love

But some are twisted
with the love of things
irreconcilable.
—Hart Crane

She would have given anything
to live the day
like an animal at his side.

The sun could die
as long as their bodies shone.
She counted on him

to lift the curse of beauty
from her eyes,
erase the edge of white

birches. But then he grew
such stubborn leaves
and she, deciduous,

lost all hers. Now
she is only at home
in a steep canyon

where the air is pure
dare. His way lies
in lime-green woods

pitched precariously
towards a moon
that knows what happened

to those candles
she lit to the saints.
They have flickered out,

their wicks dumb
as her heart wanting
this world to be enough.

A Place to Be Taken To

I cry out
as if it were my own weight

pinned
beneath the body of a day.

I slow down. I limp.
I cannot take the crush

nor table it.
You show me a woman

formed in the bowels
of a tree,

a symposium
of the motionless.

I dare not attend
her population of scars.

What if I should
find out I exist

and that Chopin is twice as sweet
as I remember him?

Wishless

I have left you with the burden
of saving my life.
You know what that means
in the Orient.

To set you free,
I've tried insanity
and other indoor sports.

Knowing
how you held me
like a chalice
you would rather give up,
I burst out
of metal and jewels
to run from you

only to stop short
on the wick of your face.

I stare at the rubber plant,
the succulents,
the Buddha's tree that survives
by luck or incense,
then close my eyes
on the first star.

Voyage to the End

I sin so much harder now
knowing what I know

a sail snaps in the wind
I look the other way

a dream is returning
from the year

of my birth
to be transfigured

like a Da Vinci smile
a nightingale

parting the leaves
a melody

the silver-green
of corn husks

pouring a river
into the sea

redeeming
the Alamos I have lost

www.ingramcontent.com/pod-product-compliance
Lightning Source LLC
La Vergne TN
LVHW010108110826
845155LV00028B/547

* 9 7 8 1 9 1 2 9 6 3 6 4 5 *